PUPPY ♥ LOVE

PUPPY ♥ LOVE

what puppies teach us about love

WILLOW CREEK PRESS

Published by Willow Creek Press
P.O. Box 147, Minocqua, Wisconsin 54548

Editor: Andrea Donner

Photo credits: p.2 © Close Encounters of the Furry Kind; p.7 © Norvia Behling; p. 8 © Brian Bevan/ardea.com; p.11 © Close Encounters of the Furry Kind; p.12, 15 © RonKimballStock.com; p.16 © Close Encounters of the Furry Kind; p.19 © Alan & Sandy Carey; p.20 © Norvia Behling; p.23 © RonKimballStock.com; p.24 © Johan De Meester/ardea.com; p.27 © Lynn Stone; p.28, 31 © RonKimballStock.com; p.32 © Larry & Marge Grant; p.35 © RonKimballStock.com; p.36 © Sue Redshaw; p.39 © Alan & Sandy Carey; p.40 © John Daniels/ardea.com; p.43 © Norvia Behling; p.44 © John Daniels/ardea.com; p.47 © Norvia Behling; p.48 © Bonnie Nance; p.51 © John Daniels/ardea.com; p.52 © RonKimballStock.com; p.55 © Norvia Behling; p.56 © RonKimballStock.com; p.59 © Norvia Behling; p.60, 63 © RonKimballStock.com; p.64 © Mitsuaki Iwago/Minden Pictures; p.67 © Lynn Stone; p. 68 © Tara Darling; p.71 © Jean Michel Labat/ardea.com; p.72 © John Daniels / ardea.com; p.75 © Gary Randall/RonKimballStock.com; p.76 © Frederic Rolland / ardea.com; p.79 © John Daniels/ardea.com; p.80 © Daniel Johnson; p.83 © Norvia Behling; p.84 © RonKimballStock.com; p.87 © Henry Groskinsky/Peter Arnold, Inc.; p.88 © Jean Michel Labat/ardea.com; p.91 © Mitsuaki Iwago/Minden Pictures; p.92 © John Daniels/ardea.com; p.95 © Nancy McCallum; p.96 © Tara Darling

Printed in Canada

First love is a little foolish and a lot of curiosity.

George Bernard Shaw

New love is exciting...

♥ ♥ ♥

The magic of first love is our
ignorance that it can ever end.

Benjamin Disraeli

It makes you giddy…

♥ ♥ ♥

To love is to receive a glimpse of heaven.

Karen Sunde

and a little crazy...

♥ ♥ ♥

There is always some madness in love.
But there is also always some reason in madness.

Friedrich Nietzsche

...and even a little sick
in the stomach.

♥ ♥ ♥

Love is a fire. But whether it is going
to warm your hearth or burn down
your house, you can never tell.

Joan Crawford

Sometimes it's awkward...

♥ ♥ ♥

The course of true love never did run smooth.

William Shakespeare

and a little scary...

♥ ♥ ♥

Love is an irresistible desire to be irresistibly desired.

Robert Frost

...and it's easy to get your
heart broken.

♥ ♥ ♥

For the memory of love is sweet,
though the love itself were in vain.

Lyster

But finding your
soulmate is the best feeling
in the world.

♥ ♥ ♥

Two souls with but a single thought,
Two hearts that beat as one.

Frederich Halm

To make love last,
be friends first.

♥ ♥ ♥

Friendship often ends in love;
but love in friendship—never.

Charles Caleb Colton

Eat together...

♥ ♥ ♥

A meal can be an erotic experience in itself.

Alex Comfort

Sleep together...

♥ ♥ ♥

I think we dream so we don't
have to be apart so long.
If we're in each other's dreams,
we can play together all night.

Bill Watterson, Calvin & Hobbes

Bathe together...

♥ ♥ ♥

Sensual pleasures are like soap bubbles,
sparkling and effervescent.

John H. Aughey

...and play together.

♥ ♥ ♥

A year, ten years from now, I'll remember this:
not why, only that we were here like this, together.

Adrienne Rich

Don't squabble over petty things...

♥ ♥ ♥

Be not the first to quarrel,
nor the last to make up.

Spanish proverb

...or put each other down.

♥ ♥ ♥

There is so much good in the worst of us,
And so much bad in the best of us,
That it ill behooves any of us,
To say anything about the rest of us.

Anonymous

Remember that feelings are easy to hurt.

♥ ♥ ♥

Maturity begins to grow when you can
sense your concern for others
outweighing your concern for yourself.

John MacNaughton

So be kind...

♥ ♥ ♥

A kind heart is a fountain of gladness, making
everything in its vicinity freshen into smiles.

Washington Irving

Be thoughtful...

♥ ♥ ♥

The fragrance always stays in the
hand that gives the rose.

Hada Bejar

Be tender...

♥ ♥ ♥

After the verb 'to Love,' 'to Help' is the
most beautiful verb in the world.

Bertha von Suttner

Be loving.

♥ ♥ ♥

A loving person lives in a loving world.
A hostile person lives in a hostile world.
Everyone you meet is your mirror.

Ken Keys

Try not to argue…

♥ ♥ ♥

The only way to get the best of
an argument is to avoid it.

Dale Carnegie

...or give each other the
silent treatment.

♥   ♥   ♥

Silence is one of the hardest
arguments to refute.

Josh Billings

Trust each other...

♥ ♥ ♥

It is impossible to go through life without trust.

Graham Greene

...and be trustworthy.

The best proof of love is trust.

Joyce Brothers

Express your feelings.

♥ ♥ ♥

The happiest moments my heart knows are those
in which it is pouring forth its affections.

Thomas Jefferson

Show affection in public.

♥ ♥ ♥

Stolen kisses require an accomplice.

Unknown

Keep your sense of humor.

♥ ♥ ♥

The most wasted of all days
is one without laughter.

e e cummings

Forgive.

♥ ♥ ♥

'Tis the most tender part of love,
each other to forgive.

John Sheffield

Go on adventures together.

♥ ♥ ♥

Life is either a daring adventure or nothing.

Helen Keller

Encourage each other.

♥ ♥ ♥

Each person has an ideal, a hope, a dream which
represents the soul. We must give to it the
warmth of love, the light of understanding and
the essence of encouragement.

Colby Dorr Dam

Support each other.

♥ ♥ ♥

Alone we can do so little;
together we can do so much.

Helen Keller

Don't keep secrets.

♥ ♥ ♥

Nothing makes us so lonely as our secrets.

Paul Tournier

Give lots of hugs...

♥ ♥ ♥

Sometimes it's better to put love into
hugs than to put it into words.

Unknown

and kisses...

♥ ♥ ♥

Soul meets soul on lovers' lips.

Percy Bysshe Shelley

...and smiles.

♥ ♥ ♥

Smile, it is the key that fits the lock
of everybody's heart.

Anthony J. D'Angelo

Be dependable.

♥ ♥ ♥

Hold faithfulness and sincerity
as first principles.

Confucius

Hold hands.

♥ ♥ ♥

Now join your hands, and with
your hands your hearts.

William Shakespeare

Laugh often.

♥ ♥ ♥

Laughter is the closest distance
between two people.

Victor Borge

Comfort each other.

♥ ♥ ♥

A good exercise for the heart is to
bend down and help another up.

Anonymous

Listen.

♥ ♥ ♥

The first duty of love is to listen.

Paul Tillich

Celebrate important events together.

♥ ♥ ♥

Age does not protect you from love. But love,
to some extent, protects you from age.

Jeanne Moreau

Lean on each other.

♥ ♥ ♥

One word frees us of all the weight
and pain of life: That word is love.

Sophocles

Don't take love for granted.

♥ ♥ ♥

There is no remedy for love but to love more.

Henry David Thoreau

Appreciate each other.

♥ ♥ ♥

Give all to love; obey thy heart.

Ralph Waldo Emerson

Cherish every day you have together.

♥ ♥ ♥

Love one another and you will be happy.
It's as simple and as difficult as that.

Michael Leunig